THE 1920s:

THE RISE OF MODERN AMERICA

BY

DAVID B. McCOY

SPARE CHANGE PRESS™
EST. 1979

Special thanks to my proofreading team: Dr. Rhonda Baughman, Mary Ann D'Aurelio. Ann McPeek, and Dave Huthmacher.

* * *

The 1920s: The Rise of Modern America
© 2014, 2018, 2019 by David B. McCoy

ISBN: 9780945568520

* * *

INTRODUCTION

The 1920s was a period of immense social, cultural, and industrial changes, making it one of the most important transition periods in American History. Many aspects of our "modern" lifestyle we take for granted arose during this decade.

The groundwork for these changes had been building for some time, but it was not until the 1920s that new technologies, the introduction of psychology, and increased urbanization would gain enough momentum to overshadow the dominant Victorian beliefs and practices of the late nineteenth century.

1920 through 1929 has been referred to as the Roaring Twenties, the Jazz Age, and the Age of Wonderful Nonsense. As might be surmised by the use of such terms, historians have generally viewed the 1920s as one in which little happened. However, by concentrating primarily on major political, diplomatic, military, and economic developments, students of history are left with an era enshrouded in myths and stereotypes.

Despite lacking the substance that catches the historian's attention, no other era in American history casts such a long shadow over the nation's collective imagination and popular culture. The intent of this publication is to revisit the 1920s and learn how and why it marks the rise of modern America. It would be impossible to cover all the changes that occurred in a publication this small, thus the focus will be on those changes that occurred during the 1920s and are still with us today.

THE SOCIOLOGICAL AND TECHNOLOGICAL PRELUDE TO THE 1920s

Most authors writing about the 1920s hint that some identifiable features of the decade's culture resulted from the nation's Second Industrial Revolution, but by-and-large, prefer to begin their chronicling of the era with the ending of World War One. However, without sociological and technological perspectives, a reader is short-changed in understanding the driving forces behind the drastic cultural changes.

People of the First Industrial Revolution were producers and consumers, with an emphasis on production. One's identity was based on what job he/she performed and what he/she produced, either by themselves or as a team of workers. People generally were inner-directed with an emphasis on personal autonomy and self-sacrifice. These ideals were expressed and reinforced by Horatio Alger who wrote more than one hundred success stories which asserted hard work, sobriety, thrift, and restraint as the keys to personal and business good fortune.

Before the twentieth century, most manufactured products were made individually by hand. A craftsman would use his skills and tools, such as files, knives, and chisels to create individual parts. He would then assemble the individual parts into the final product. In the late nineteenth century, when manufacturers embraced electrically run machines over those steam driven, and the ideas of the interchangeable parts and division of labor, there were dramatic gains in productivity. Eventually, however, the demand for skilled craftsmen began to decline.

Also in the late 1900s, a theory of management intended to maximize labor productivity and economic efficiency was developed by Frederick W. Taylor. He believed work could be made scientific by standardizing the steps each worker performed: there was one best (standard) way to perform each job, one best (standard) tool to perform it with, and a stipulated (standard) amount of time in which to complete the job. His "scientific management" greatly increased the productivity of factories, but at the same time further undercut the need for skilled laborers.

The impact of these innovations changed the nature of work in four important ways. First, tasks were minutely subdivided and performed by unskilled or semiskilled workers. Second, this new method of manufacturing necessitated the formation of a hierarchy of supervisors and managers (thus causing workers to lose autonomy) as factories not only grew in size, but as companies expanded across the country. Third, the increasing complexity of operations gave rise to managerial-level employees who specialized in accounting, research and development, distribution, marketing, and sales, but had no part in production. Finally, it led to a split between production and consumption.

As the Second Industrial Revolution evolved, with its interchangeable parts, division of labor, and automated assembly lines, those workers who had formerly been self-sufficient were reduced to being "small cogs in the large wheel" of manufacturing. What previous identification and pride workers had become intrinsically less meaningful. Consequently, Americans came to judge themselves, and each other, based not on their strength of character or job but rather on which brand-name products they purchased and what they did during their leisure time.

In addition to the sociological changes occurring, it is also noteworthy to recognize a few technological innovations that made the 1920s possible. The Second Industrial Revolution is usually dated between the latter half of the nineteenth century until World War One. It is considered to have begun in 1865 with the introduction of the Henry Bessemer steel converter in the United States in 1865. Before Bessemer's process, steel was made only through a costly and arduous process by artisans who created smelt. The Bessemer process revolutionized steel manufacturing by decreasing its cost, along with greatly increasing the scale and speed of production. Cheap steel soon found many uses by 1880 which included buildings (skyscrapers), ships, machines, and railroad tracks. By the 1920s, steel was being used for automobiles, light fixtures, vacuum cleaners, ice boxes (early refrigerators), stoves, sewing machines, electric toaster, waffle irons, curling irons, etc.

Chemistry also began its journey toward the supply of new artificial materials. One that would drastically change the fashion industry was rayon. Rayon is a by-product of wood which is chemically changed and extruded in fibers that are twisted into threads and woven. It can imitate the feel and texture of silk, wool, cotton, and linen. The fibers are easily dyed in a wide range of colors. The first commercial scale production of a manufactured fiber was achieved by French chemist Count Hilaire de Chardonnet. In 1889, his fabrics of "artificial silk" caused a sensation at the Paris Fashion Exhibition. Two years later, he built the first commercial rayon plant at Besancon, France, and secured his fame as the "father of the rayon industry." Several attempts to produce "artificial silk" in the United States were made during the early 1900s but none were commercially successful until the American Viscose Company began production in 1910. DuPont

Chemicals acquired the rights to the process in the 1920s and quickly turned rayon into a household name.

A YouTube video:
"Synthetic Fibers: Nylon and Rayon (1949) Encyclopaedia Britannica Film"

In 1869, the American, John Wesley Hyatt, succeeded in creating the first synthetic plastic which he called celluloid. Its economic importance was initially modest because of its inflammability, and was primarily used for combs, knife handles, piano keys, baby rattles, and costume jewelry. From the late 1880s, cellulose nitrate was used as a film base in photography, X-ray films, and motion picture films.

In 1925, Clarence Birdseye would use cellophane packages for his new quick-freeze foods. (Cellophane is a thin, transparent sheet made of regenerated cellulose.) Another breakthrough in synthetic materials came in 1907 when the Belgian-born

American inventor, Leo Baekeland, discovered bakelite. Bakelite was particularly suitable for the emerging electrical and automobile industries because of its extraordinarily high resistance, not only to electricity, but to heat and chemical action. It was soon used for all nonconducting parts of electric motors, radios, telephone casings, automobile distributor caps, and other electrical devices, such as bases and sockets for light bulbs and vacuum tubes.

Like chemistry, the economic potential of electricity had been suspected since the beginning of the nineteenth century. By 1882, New Jersey inventor, Thomas A. Edison, opened the first electric generating station in Manhattan. He was able to provide power to streetcars, factories, and private homes, but his use of direct currents limited the distance in which power could be supplied—only about one and a quarter miles from the power source. It would take until Nikola Tesla developed an electric motor using the system of alternating current to solve the "line loss" problem. By using Tesla's AC current, factory owners were soon able to automate assembly lines which led to mass production.

An explanation of AC vs DC power, and line loss, can be found at YouTube:
"AC vs DC ScienceOnline," first video.

A fair question to ask is "If the mentioned factors were so important, why didn't the rise of a modern society occur until the 1920s?" Some changes did, in fact, begin to appear in the early years of the 20th century, but the nation was drawn into the First World War. As so often happens in time of war, the home front of the United States saw a systematic mobilization of the entire population and the entire economy to produce the soldiers, food supplies, munitions, and money needed to win the war. Then after the war, because President Woodrow Wilson was not only mentally and physically incapacitated his last two years in office, when he was lucid, he was more concerned with his League of Nations. Consequently, his administration made no provisions for returning soldiers and simply cancelled all war contracts. These two missteps threw the country into a recession that lasted until Henry Ford sparked a revolution in transportation. By the mid-1920s, one of eight U.S. workers was somehow involved in the production, sales, service, and fueling of automobiles. (The overall impact will be explored in deal in the next section.)

Another reason change accelerated during the 1920s is that for the first time more people were living in urban areas than on farms or small villages. A city's size itself conferred anonymity on its residents. Individuals could decide with whom to associate and how to behave. With all the congestion, tumult, hustle, and bustle of the modern metropolis, no community overseers could keep track of, much less reward or punish, people's behavior. Thus, old order Puritan/Victorian moral customs gave way to the new order of the urban life.

THE AUTOMOBILE: PART ONE

No technological advancement transformed American life during the 1920s more than the automobile. The automobile was to the 1920s what television would be to the 1950s and computers and the Internet to the 1990s. Although primitive gasoline-powered "horseless carriages" had been manufactured in the United States since the mid-1890s, the 1920s marked the first decade in which automobile ownership became common among ordinary Americans. The individual most responsible for putting so many Americans behind the wheel was Henry Ford.

In 1906 Ford began building a reliable four-cylinder, fifteen-horse powered, middle-class car, the $600 Model N. (What cost $600.00 in 1906 would cost $15,096.92 today.). Then in 1908 Ford announced, "I will build a car for the great multitude. It will be large enough for the family, but small enough for the individual to run and care for. It will be constructed of the best materials, by the best men to be hired, after the simplest designs that modern engineering can devise. But it will be so low in price that no man making a good salary will be unable to own one — and enjoy with his family the blessing of hours of pleasure in God's great open spaces." By the next year, Ford released his Model T.

In 1913, Ford incorporated Taylor's "scientific management" techniques into his production line, creating a system based on interchangeable parts and a division of labor in which each employee repeatedly performed only small, simple tasks that minimized time and effort. Ford also installed moving assembly lines, which allowed chassis, and other automotive parts, to flow continuously from one station to the next through his new 65-acre Highland Park Plant near Detroit, Michigan. Consequently, the cost of manufacturing the Model T was dramatically reduced from $850.00 in 1909 ($21,394.41) to $290.00 ($7,299.00) in 1924.

While Henry Ford was opening the mass market of automobiles, William C. Durant was buying up numerous auto manufacturing companies, including Buick, Oldsmobile, Cadillac, and Chevrolet to create General Motors. The first and most influential GM innovation was its introduction of consumer credit. Before the late 1910s, purchasing an automobile required immediate cash payment. Within two years of GM's establishment of the General Motors Acceptance Corporation (GMAC) in 1919, half of all automobiles were financed; by 1926 the figure reached three-fourths.

Credit buying not only drastically enlarged the number of people who could afford the initial cost of an automobile, it also altered their buying habits. Ford sought to attract customers with a low-price product, one simple and durable enough to last a very long time. The Model T's unchanged, black appearance and longevity was a great part of its appeal; however, it would not take long for the public to want sleeker and more stylish cars.

Innovations that began to be offered by Ford's main competitors, GM and Chrysler, were a wide selection of eye-catching colors; foot, instead of hand-operated, brakes; hardtop enclosures for the driver and passengers; roll-up windows; self, instead of hand-crank, starters; automatic windshield wipers, and more. Ford would lag behind these types of innovations until he introduced his Model A in 1927.

Alfred P. Sloan became president and chief executive officer of GM in 1923 shortly after Durant lost control of GM. Sloan transformed GM from the loose cluster of business units into an archetype of the modern business enterprise. One of his first steps was to establish a pricing "ladder of success" structure, from lowest to highest: from Chevrolet ... to Pontiac ... to Oldsmobile ... to Buick ... with Cadillac at the top. Under this scheme, Sloan put in place a system predicated on buyers' evident motivation to "move up" to a superior model every few years.

And since new technology did not emerge every year to provide a fresh incentive for the purchase of a new car, other means had to be found. This time, Sloan decided to appear to people's vanity by annually redesigning car fenders and dashboards which proved neither difficult nor expensive, yet provided a means of distinguishing each year's model from earlier models. From these annual styling changes came the concept of planned obsolescence. To carry this out, readers of newspapers and magazines were bombarded by large display ads with cleverly crafted texts and pictures. This marketing strategy emphasized cosmetic changes in the outer appearance of each year's model and encouraged owners to trade their still-serviceable cars for more stylish new ones. Through such messages, people came to believe that by owning the newest model it would bestow upon them a higher social status or increased sex appeal.

THE AUTOMOBILE: PART TWO

Automobile production played a significant role in fueling the nation's economy by stimulating the growth and development of a network of related industries, including steel, petroleum, glass, and rubber manufacturing. Tractors and motorized trucks, an offshoot of the automobile industry, revolutionized agriculture.

The number of gas-powered tractors jumped by 26% by 1930, and the expanded use of motorized farming equipment dramatically boosted the nation's agricultural output.

Soaring automobile sales also accelerated the expansion and development of American highways and government spending. In 1921, Congress passed the Federal Highway Act which provided states matching federal funds in order to finance the construction of a network of two-lane, hard-surface roads. This in turn stimulated an entire roadside service industry of filling stations, auto repair garages, campgrounds, motels, and restaurants.

Automobiles also created new leisure activities for many Americans. On weekends, families ventured into the countryside to go camping, picnicking, sightseeing, or visiting. Family automobile vacations also became a common facet of middle-class American life. For American youth, automobiles represented new freedoms. Teens came to use automobiles as a means of escaping parental authority, especially when it came to dating and courtship. As a result, dating moved from the front porch to the back seat. Also, driving around for the sheer please of it, called joyriding, became a popular pastime.

As might be expected, conservative leaders condemned the automobile for eroding the cohesion of American families and morally corrupting the nation's youth. Ministers railed on about the desecration of the Sabbath as some members of their congregations went out for Sunday drives rather than attending church services. However, Americans had become too attached to their automobiles to be swayed by such priggish pronouncements.

ELECTRICITY

Electricity, while not a new phenomenon, came to influence the daily lives of Americans during the 1920s. Pre-electric life had a different rhythm, feel, and even smell. Light produced from wood, coal, candle, or petroleum was dim, smoky, and smelly. Its grime and odor permeated a home in which even regular strenuous cleaning could not eliminate. And for the most part, lives were governed by the rising and setting of the sun.

The widespread use of electricity literally empowered people to redesign the basic schedule of their daily existence. Electric light made it possible to live conveniently by the clock instead of by daily and seasonal fluctuations. Also the nature of work, particularly in the industrial sector, was dramatically affected. Electricity could drive small motors, reducing the need for elaborate systems of drive shafts, gears, and belts linking every factory mechanism to the central power source. Electric current could propel assembly lines for the automobile industry and made possible other mass-produced goods.

Domestic use of electricity was for the most part devoted to lighting. For a while, natural gas replaced candle and petroleum lamps within cities. The gas light was simply the light of a naked gas flame and looked much like a large candle flame. Its introduction made a large difference because light became readily available without the need to continually clean and trim the wicks of oil lamps, or the constant need to replace candles and clean up spilled wax. However, gas lighting made rooms very hot and stuffy by taking oxygen from the air. Furthermore, the relative inflexibility of gas pipes, and dangers associated with leaking pipes, put natural gas at a disadvantage. As a result, the gas industry began concentrating its efforts on the improvements of gas cooking stoves, water heaters, and hot air furnaces.

The adopted transmission of AC current at 120 volts by 1910, and a significant reduction in the price of electricity, encouraged the mass production of electrical products. After lights, the electric irons were at the top of the list for most homeowners. No longer did users have to turn on (or fire up with wood) the stove which would be used to heat a metal iron. In the age before air-conditioning, electric fans also came into high demand. Other products that soon found their way into homes were vacuum cleaners, ice boxes (early refrigerators), stoves, sewing machines, electric toasters, waffle irons, etc.

Home appliances altered the nature of women's work but scarcely eliminated it. The increased availability of electric appliances appears to have caused greater expectations regarding domestic conditions. Better and more varied meals, cleaner houses, and more frequently laundered clothing all came to be considered normal.

It did not take long for architects and builders to take advantage of electricity's adaptability and relative safety. However, electric wiring added substantially to the cost of house construction. To keep prices stable while adding electricity and indoor plumbing, builders began designing houses with open interior plans in which living rooms, dining rooms, and kitchens flowed together. The only isolated and private spaces were bedrooms and bathrooms. Single-purpose rooms such as libraries, pantries, sewing rooms, and spare bedrooms, which had comprised the Victorians' sense of uniqueness and complex domestic life, disappeared. The most widespread manifestation of this new home design was the bungalow.

Bungalows had a box-like design and were usually built in a single story, often with a single upper room or attic under a gently pitched roof. Simple, informal, and intended to be sparsely furnished, the bungalow was quickly proclaimed to be the new standard of sensible and thrifty family living. At the height of the style's popularity, several companies even sold bungalow kits through mail-order catalogs. All the building components (e.g., pre-cut lumber, nails, doors, plumbing) were delivered to the construction site, where local craftsmen erected the homes according to kit instructions. The bungalow style would dominate home building until after World War II and the introduction of the ranch house.

Electricity also transformed urban transportation. By the turn of the twentieth century, intricate networks of electric streetcars—also called trolley cars—ran from outlying neighborhoods to downtown offices and department stores. A few large cities moved their streetcars far above street level, creating elevated or "el" trains. Other cities, like New York, Boston, and Philadelphia built subways by moving their rail lines underground. These streetcars, elevated trains, and subways enabled cities to annex suburban developments that mushroomed along the advancing highway transportation routes.

Finally, as late as the 1890s, there had scarcely been such a thing as an urban nightlife. Once the sun set, towns and cities could rely only on gas lamps which cast a short and dim glow. Inhabitants were warned of "the fearful mysteries of darkness in the metropolis—the festivities of prostitution, the orgies of pauperism, the haunts of theft and murder, the scenes of drunkenness and beastly debauch" (see David Nasaw, 1999). Then the combination of Tesla's AC current and Thomas Edison's incandescent bulb transformed cities from dark and treacherous places into glittering multicolored wonderlands. Electric street lamps illuminated not only the area immediately around lampposts, but both sides of the streets with clear and bright white light.

These new illuminated streets provided city residents with an incentive to leave their darkened or gas-lit apartments to go out "when all the shop fronts [were] lighted, and the entrances to the theaters blaze[d] out on the sidewalk like open fireplaces" (see David Nasaw, 1999). The lighting of city lights would soon come to signal that the workday was over and the time for play had begun.

ADVERTISING

After several millennia of being producers, people suddenly found they had become primarily consumers. Before, what people produced, or did for a living, was how they classified themselves. But with mass production, and with its production lines, interchangeable parts, and divisions of labor, people were left with no recognizable self-identity. Realizing this, advertisers saw their opportunity to convince Americans that the vehicle for replacing this new void was to be found in the mass-produced goods available in the nation's new department stores, chain stores, and mail-order catalogs.

Unlike advertisements of the late nineteenth century which primarily sought to inform consumers of a particular product's features and availability, by the 1920s ads created associations between a product and such desirable traits as youthfulness, attractiveness, intelligence, and popularity. Other admen willfully embraced the teaching of the turn-of-the century psychologist, G. Stanly Hall, who wrote "Everyone, especially those who lead the drab life of the modern toiler, needs and craves an occasional 'good time.' Indeed, we all need to glow, tingle, and feel life intensely now and then." In their ads, they emphasized the happiness and exhilaration that came from buying their soap, their automobile, or their clothing. Unwittingly, it would be during the 1920s that Americans increasingly came to define themselves through the houses, cars, clothes, and other goods and services they purchased.

Admen and retailers were aware that while men were usually primary wage earners in families, women did most of the actual purchasing. As a result, female consumers became the main focus for everything from food products, to kitchen and cleaning appliances. Companies promised that buying their product would streamline meal preparation or lighten wives' domestic workload. Other ads suggested that buying a certain product would make them better wives and mothers.

Admen also helped to fuel the trend of worshiping youthfulness in all its forms. Fashions, particularly women's fashions, emphasized a slim, youthful figure, and the cosmetics industry exploded as women proved willing to try any product that promised to prevent or even reverse the aging process. Some cosmetic companies even urged women to "Find Yourself" through the application of makeup. Whereas Victorian moralists claimed that lipstick and a slavish attention to fashion masked one's true inner self, the new message was that lipstick and stylish clothes empowered the superwoman beneath the skin.

With the new desire to maintain a slender profile, Lucky Strike Cigarettes ran ads which, in bold type, read: *Light a Lucky and you'll never miss sweets that make you fat. And then in small type: Instead of eating between meals...instead of*

fattening sweets...beautiful women keep youthful slenderness these days by smoking Luckies. La-Mar Laboratories ran an ad claiming: *Wash away fat and years of age with La-Mar reducing soap. No dieting or exercising. Acts like magic in reducing double chin, abdomen, ungainly ankles, unbecoming wrists, arms, and shoulders, large busts, or superfluous fat on body.*

Certainly, one of the most creative ads at the time was for the dangers of "halitosis." The Lambert Pharmaceutical Company manufactured a solution used to clean cuts and scrapes and as a household antiseptic, floor cleaner, and cure for gonorrhea. Then a member of the Lambert research team happened across the word "halitosis," an obscure medical term for bad breath, in a British newspaper. When it was confirmed that there was no ill harm done by swirling a small dose of their Listerine in one's mouth, the company's president instructed his admen to market Listerine as the only proven cure for the serious medical and social disease: bad breath. Ads carried photos of forlorn young women with captions that read: *Halitosis makes you unpopular; She never knew why (her love left her for another woman); They talk behind your back—and rightly so, halitosis is inexcusable.*

And "so it went with all sorts of new disorders—dandruff, athlete's foot, body order, face wrinkles, dry or oily hair, acne, rough skin. Beneath every imperfection lurked a disastrous end—a lost job, a lost love, a missed opportunity. And for every danger, there was a cure—a new face cream, antiseptic, soap, shade of lipstick, or hair tonic to ward off the looming threat of social failure. By the end of the decade, annual sales of toiletries and beauty services had mushroomed, and the volume of advertising for toiletries ranked second only to food" (Joshua Zeitz, 2006).

In their study of modern American culture, Robert and Helen Lynd, at the time noted it was naïve to underestimate the impact advertising was having on the rise of subjective standards. They saw popular magazines and national advertising write a type of copy which made readers emotionally uneasy by insinuating "decent people" didn't live the way they did. And with inexpensive mass-produced products, the advent of installment buying, and growing need to present their best image, the people of the 1920s splurged. Ironically though, in their yearning to find their unique identity, Americans helped create a standardized modern American culture.

FASHIONS

At the dawn of the twentieth century, woman's fashion transitioned from the popular "hourglass" figure to dresses designed with an "S" curve. This style, often referred to as the Gibson Girl Look, was intended to show off the woman's figure and highlight delicate curves. When laced even moderately tightly, the S-bend corset pushed the abdomen back, threw the breasts forward and arched the back. A corset cover was worn over a corset and it buttoned up the front. It would be made of lightweight cotton and would hide the corset seams that might otherwise be visible through a blouse or dress.

Women's skirts and dresses came down to the floor or sometimes as high as the ankle. A walking skirt was a simple everyday style of skirt that was wide enough at the bottom for walking or riding a bicycle. A blouse, also known as a "shirtwaist," was tailored to include some details similar to men's shirts. Often times, shirtwaists were made of linen and decorated with machine-stitched embroidery. The stand-up collar style was common on most shirtwaists. A belt, made of cloth or leather, with a buckle was usually worn with a shirtwaist. Women's shoes had thick heels and pointed toes. They might slip on, button or lace and came above or below the ankle.

An interactive Flash display of this type of clothing can be found at <www.americancenturies.mass.edu/activities/dressup/notflash/1900_woman.html>

The First World War (1914-1918) had a pronounced effect on women's fashion in the Western world. Fabrics and materials used for clothing were scarce, and clothing became simpler and less ornamented as a result. Perhaps the biggest impact was on women's hemlines. Prior to the war they had risen from floor to ankle length, then jumped to mid-calf length by war's end. The war also brought more women into the workplace which led to the wearing of once-forbidden trousers, and even a tendency for female office workers to wear feminized versions of men's suits and shirts.

Several events and technological developments occurred to allow a major transformation in women's fashions during the 1920s. First was the emergence in France of the fashion designer Coco Chanel. Her designs eliminated the frills and excesses of women's couture in favor of styles that offered comfort, maneuverability, and practical use. By throwing off the corset she achieved an uninterrupted flow between the torso and the chest, thereby creating a new silhouette.

Coco Chanel

Chanel's signature style culminated sometime around 1923 in what was called the "garcoone (little boy) look" or simply the "flapper look." It featured one-piece garments that hung from the shoulders in a straight line past the waists and hips to the hem. The straight line from the shoulders to hem was interrupted by either a seam or decorated at the hip line. It was simple line without the elaborate seaming or darting as used in fitted garments, but was highly decorated with quilting, tucking, tiny pleats, gatherings, and intricate decorative beading. Most dresses were also embellished with bows, belts, buttons, ribbons, brooches, fringe, feathers, and even fur.

Second was in the introduction of artificial silk. This was a man-made fabric known as viscose rayon. This new fabric had the drapability and sheen of silk, but was less expensive, required less care, and could be combined with cotton and wool. Artificial silk was also a material designers could easily imprint exotic and art deco patterns. Rayon was widely available to both home seamstresses and manufacturing companies enabling them to construct the new fluid dresses without the use of expensive silk.

Third, as noted before, for the first time in American history, the majority of people were living in urban areas. Women in large numbers were becoming domestic servants, secretaries, telephone operators, typists, department store clerks, teachers, nurses and social workers. Consequently, clothes that were simple in cut, inexpensive, and meeting the needs of motion in the workplace, came into high demand.

Fourth, was the development of ready-made clothing and inexpensive paper sewing patterns. Machine-made, mass-produced clothing become common in the late nineteenth century but only for men's clothing. Most women's and children's clothing continued to be made at home. Then, with the simplicity of sewing straight, unfitting garments, men's clothing manufacturers quickly expanded their production to include off-the-rack, ready-to-wear women's clothing. Home sewing also became more popular among less wealthy women because of the one-piece style. Paper patterns were available to home sewers and local dress makers from such companies as Butterick, Home, Vogue, and McCall's.

The fashion of "bobbed" hair became another center element of the flapper style. Not only did extremely short-cropped hair emphasize the slender look, it served as another break with tradition. During the nineteenth century, long hair was a standard of beauty with hair regarded as a woman's crowning glory. The new bob style could be worn with or without bangs and was often accompanied by side curls plastered to the cheek or by a single curl dramatically set in the middle of the forehead. Around 1923, the standard bob cut began to evolve into different, even shorter styles. The shingle or "boyish bob," tapered to a point at the nape of the neck, often featured waves or short curls on the sides. The even more radical "Eton crop," was trimmed above the wearer's ears and shaved in the back. Yet, while popular concepts of the Roaring Twenties suggest every fashionable woman bobbed her hair, many women did keep their long hair. And by the end of the decade, the ubiquitous bob cut gave way to women wearing more convenient and slightly longer bobbed styles.

The new flapper-style brought with it changes in how women were viewed by society. The new androgynous look, with its boyish and linear figure—often achieved with the help of a breast flattener that de-accentuated all traces of feminine lines—suggested that men's and women's roles were bleeding into each other. Furthermore, through history, clothing has been an identifiable means of distinguishing a person's social class. However, the introduction of dress patterns, rayon fabric, and ready-to wear clothing, helped create, at least in appearance, a society of equals.

MOTION PICTURES: PART ONE
Adapted from History of Cinema in USA, Filmbirth.com

In the late 1880s, Thomas Edison and his assistant, William Dickson, developed the Kinetophonograph (or Kinetophone), a precursor of the 1891 Kinetoscope, that synchronized film *projection* with sound from a phonograph record. The projector was connected to the phonograph with a pulley system, but it didn't work very well and was difficult to synchronize. Although Edison is often credited with the development of early motion picture cameras and projectors, it was Dickson, in November 1890, who devised a crude *camera*, called a Kinetograph, which could photograph motion pictures.

The motor-driven camera was designed to capture movement with a synchronized shutter and sprocket system that could move the film through the camera by an electric motor. The Kinetograph used film 35mm wide and had sprocket holes to advance the film. The sprocket system would momentarily pause the film roll before the camera's shutter to create a photographic frame (a still or photographic image). The formal introduction of the Kinetograph in October of 1892 set the standard for theatrical motion picture cameras throughout the twentieth century.

YouTube video:
"Edison's Kinetoscope. Museu del Cinema"

Early spectators in Kinetoscope parlors were amazed by even the most mundane 30 and 60 seconds moving images of approaching trains colliding, parades, women dancing, dogs terrorizing rats, and twisting contortionists. In the early 1900s, motion pictures ("flickers") were no longer innovative experiments. They soon became a popular entertainment medium for the working-class masses, where one could spend an evening at the cinema for a cheap entry fee. Kinetoscope parlors, lecture halls, and storefronts were often converted into nickelodeons, the first real movie theaters. The normal admission charge was a nickel, sometimes a dime, hence the name nickelodeon.

Films really blossomed in the 1920s, expanding upon the foundations of film from earlier years. Most U.S. film production at the start of the decade occurred in or near Hollywood on the West Coast, although some films were still being made in New Jersey and on Long Island. By the mid-20s, movies were big business, with a capital investment totaling over $2 billion dollars. By the end of the decade, there were twenty Hollywood studios, and the demand for films was greater than ever. Most people are unaware that the greatest output of feature films in the U.S. occurred in the 1920s and 1930s, averaging about 800 film releases a year. Nowadays, it is remarkable when production exceeds 500 films in a year.

Throughout most of the decade, silent films were the predominant product of the film industry, with films becoming bigger, costlier, and more polished. They were manufactured assembly-line style in Hollywood's 'entertainment factories,' in which production was broken down and organized into its various writing, costuming, sets, makeup, and directing components.

Even the earliest films were organized into genres or types, with instantly recognizable storylines, settings, costumes, and characters. The major genre emphasis was on swashbucklers, historical extravaganzas, and melodramas, although all kinds of films were being produced throughout the decade. Films varied from sexy melodramas and biblical epics by Cecil B. DeMille, to westerns, horror films, gangster/crime films, war films, romances, mysteries, and comedies.

By the mid-1920s, the art of silent film had become remarkably mature. Although called silent, they were never really silent but accompanied by sound organs, gramophone discs, musicians, sound effects specialists, live actors who delivered dialogue, and even full-scale orchestras. There would be two competing sound or recording systems developed during the early 'talkie' period: sound-on-disc and sound-on-film.

In 1925-26, America technologically revolutionized the entire industry when Warner Brothers, with Bell Telephone researchers, developed a revolutionary synchronized sound system called Vitaphone. This process allowed sound to be recorded on a phonograph record (sound-on-disc) that was electronically linked and synchronized with the film projector—but it was destined to be faulty due to inherent synchronization problems. It did not take long for the Vitaphone to be replaced by a strip of celluloid prepped for sound that ran down the side of the film strip (sound-on-film), so that the two modes remain in sync.

The sound era was officially inaugurated when audiences heard vaudeville star, Al Jolson, improvise a song's introduction: "Wait a minute! Wait a minute! You ain't heard nothin' yet," after the film's first musical interlude. Jolson proved his boast by continuing to sing *Toot, Toot, Tootsie*. They were further astonished by his talking to his mother in an extemporaneous way after singing *Blue Skies*, and the film's final song *Mammy*.

MOTION PICTURES: PART TWO

By 1923, the United States had 15,000 silent movie theaters with an average capacity of 507 seats and a weekly attendance of 50 million views. Attendance would more than double over the next seven years, making movies a normal feature of life. It would also become the fifth largest industry during the decade. With better quality films, the audiences shifted from nearly all working class to increasingly middle and upper classes, and so too did the settings of stories. Increasingly, movies showed actors and actresses (except westerns or tramp/hobo films) wearing evening clothes, living in elegant homes, and passing time in cabarets. Films of this sort encouraged audiences to think of material opulence as widespread, which reinforced ideals of consumption as seen in popular movie and other wide-circulating magazines. In a powerful way, movies provided Americans with a unifying cultural experience—regardless of what section of the nation they lived or their socioeconomic status. Viewers saw the same movies, admired the same stars, and imitated their dress, mannerisms, behaviors, and hairstyles.

The youth of the 1920s were the first generation to learn their manners and morals from movies, and the lessons learned were not always acceptable to people with older, rural values. The movies' emphasis on sex, along with several personal scandals involving screen stars, led conservative groups to force studio heads to establish such rules as "two feet on the floor" for bedroom scenes.

In such films as *It*, which can be seen at YouTube by typing "It 1927 movie," the free-spirited, and apparently sexually liberated Clara Bow, demonstrated a chaste goodness under her haughty behavior in order to win her man. In the 1920 film, *Why Change Your Wife?* (also on YouTube), the beautiful Gloria Swanson portrayed a frumpy housewife who was losing her husband to a glamorous, well made-up and dressed interloper. Swanson responds by buying a flapper wardrobe of sexy sleeveless, black dresses interwoven with gold and feathers and, of course, wins her husband back. On one level the films conveyed the triumph of conventional virtues, but on another level, demonstrated that married as well as single women needed to pay attention to their appearances.

COURTSHIP AND MARRIAGE

Perhaps, the most noteworthy aspect in creating our modern society related to courtship and marriage. In the Victorian era, women and men inhabited a world largely segregated by gender. Men worked and women ideally attended to childrearing and domestic work. Men socialized at the saloon or private club while women passed their free hours at one another's home. For men, sexual intercourse was a necessary release; for women, it was a duty. Men smoked cigars and cigarettes, but in Victorian society, only women of dubious character smoked. However, by the end of World War One, with urban growth, technological innovations, and new consumption-minded advertising, stubborn Victorian ways of life began to falter.

*   *   *

Courtship, the process of identifying and engaging a life partner, changed most dramatically after World War One. Before, Victorian era courtship took place in the home according to well-defined customs. A young man would "call" on a young woman and in doing so, he would meet her parents. The couple would talk in the family parlor, perhaps be offered refreshments, and ultimately be encouraged to call again or be discouraged from doing so. If the courtship progresses, the couple might move from the parlor to the still visible front porch. They might even attend public functions together, and only when a young lady felt comfortable with her suitor, consent to privately go for a buggy ride. Then by the 1920s, a new sort of freedom was made possible by the automobile. It offered an almost universally available means of escaping temporarily from the supervision of parents and chaperones. And with new hardtop enclosures for the driver and passengers, the automobile became, in effect, a room protected from the weather which could be occupied at any time of the day or night and could be moved into a darkened byway or a country lane.

As long as females lived in their parents' home, women were in control of the courting process: they did the inviting; they set the hours and day of the visit, and they set the limits on physical contact. However, when women moved to urban areas to live and work, courting ceased to be just a search for a mate, and the concept of dating emerged. In large cities, between one-quarter and one-third of working women lived alone in private apartments or boarding houses.

Electrifications and mechanization caused a 72 percent increase in the amount of production per worker, and a drop in the number of hours the typical American worked. And with this, wages, particularly for men, rose to $29.39 with women earning about $17.36 a week. With a large unmarried population, more free time, money, and cities lit all night long, dating became the primary male-female social entertainment. Regretfully, though, the discrepancy in wages between men and women, placed men, who had more money, in control of the dating process.

A central component of the new dating system was "treating," whereby a young man paid for dinner, drinks at a speakeasy, a movie, a dance or other amusement. In return the young lady provided lively companionship, and commonly physical affection known as "petting," which consisted of kissing, hugging, and caressing of varying intensity just short of intercourse. As might be expected, advice columns frequently printed letters from girls bemoaning the fact that without petting they could not keep a boyfriend. Despite this, intercourse was generally confined to engaged couples as a prelude to marriage. Yet, for many women, as for men, the new system was often exciting. As one Ohio State coed proclaimed, "The girl with sport in her blood ... gets by. She kisses the boys, she smokes with them, drinks with them, and why? Because the feeling of comradeship is running rampant."

Two activities, just a few years prior, that would have been unheard of were women drinking and smoking. Thanks to the 1920s Prohibition, male dominated saloons were closed only to give rise to speakeasies.

Speakeasies were hidden sections of an establishment used to illegally sell alcoholic beverages. In most cases, a password, specific handshake or secret knock was required to enter. Besides liquor, many provided food, floor shows, and live bands playing jazz to which people danced the new craze, the Charleston. These new nightspots became a favorite haunt for dating singles living in cities. For both men and women, cocktails became fashionable because bootleg liquor needed to be sweet and highly flavored to mask its venomous taste. Like drinking illegal alcohol, women began smoking cigarettes as a public display of both their equality with men and their emancipation from Victorian codes of behavior. Promoters of

Lucky Strike cigarettes deliberately linked smoking with female emancipation by calling cigarettes "Torches of Liberty."

* * *

While it is true the flapper challenged prevailing notions about gender roles, demanded the same social freedoms as men, flouted conventionality, drank in speakeasies, doubled the nation's consumption of cigarettes, and flirted openly, she also began to view marriage as a partnership of equals, with the possibility of happiness and satisfaction. The notion emerged that a compassionate marriage succeeded because of mutual devotion, sexual attraction, and respect for spousal equality. Furthermore, no marriage could be free from tension or conflict, but husbands and wives who were loving companions could communicate and resolve difficulties.

The possibility of happiness and satisfaction within marriage also found its way into the bedroom. The Victorian moral code did not permit women to admit to a sexual appetite, but the growing public assumption was that sex was a vital part of a good marriage. A major influence on this new thinking came from Freudian psychologists. They explained human motivation as primarily sexual in origin, and thus removed individuals the burden of guilt, anxiety, and repression. Understandably, women quickly embraced the idea that sexual relations were not simply a means of procreation or a duty, but a pleasurable experience and culmination of romantic love. And the legitimacy of female sexuality was advanced by the increasing availability of birth control devices, especially after 1925 when diaphragms were first manufactured in the United States.

INDOOR LEISURE ACTIVITIES

RADIO

The radio, first invented in 1895 by Guglielmo Marconi, was originally used more for communication than for entertainment. Even after Lee DeForrest's improved electronic triode vacuum tube, replacing crystal sets which could only pick up stations within a limited range, radio was slow to catch on. DeForrest's triode tube made possible amplified radio technology and long-distance telecommunication. Triodes were widely used in consumer electronic devices such as radios and televisions until the 1970s, when transistors replaced them.

In 1920, radio finally came of age, beginning with the first licensed radio station, WDKA in Pittsburgh, Pennsylvania on November 4, 1920. Within two years, there were 576 licensed radio stations in business. Seen mainly as a source of free entertainment for the public, the industry continued to grow rapidly throughout the decade. An important factor in its growth was that the entire cost of broadcasting was funded by advertising.

Unlike movies, radio came to be regarded as a source of both mass entertainment and news, thus affecting how people understood their world. It influenced how people spent their leisure hours, what products they purchased, how their music tastes developed, and even how they talked. While listening to the radio was usually a private activity, neighbors and friends often gathered around a family's radio in the evening for what they called "radio parties." Young people often times moved furniture out of the way to dance to the latest jazz tunes. It was not unusual for families to spend Sunday mornings listening to nationally famous preachers and church services.

In the early days of radio, music constituted the single most popular form of station programming. During the 1920s, classical music dominated the airways, but eventually popular music, particularly jazz, filled daily broadcasting schedules. Rather than recorded music, stations generally featured live music performed in their studios. By 1924, many stations also aired "remote" broadcasts of bands and orchestras performing in concert halls and hotel ballrooms.

Besides music and advertisements, stations provided local and national news, stock and farm market reports, weather reports, political speeches, public lectures, and sports events and scores. By the late 1920s, networks offered more innovation and sophisticated programming, including westerns, detective shows, soap operas, comedies, children's shows, variety shows, and daytime shows geared to the housewife.

The first serial radio program, launched in 1929, was the *Amos 'n' Andy*, a 15-minute weekly show in which two white men (Freeman Gosden and Charles Correll) acted the parts of two black operators of a taxicab company in Chicago. Although the characters on the show seem insultingly stereotypical by today's standards, the show was hugely popular with both white and black radio audiences, with theaters often having to interrupt movie and push a radio on to the stage for the evening broadcast (Encyclopædia Britannica, 2013).

Motion pictures, and radio in particular, contributed to the standardization of American popular culture by quickly disseminating the latest songs, dances, fads, and catchphrases across the nation. Americans from every region, racial and ethnic group, and income level shared common experiences that helped to bring a diverse nation of people closer together.

MAGAZINES

Readers purchased popular magazines devoted to almost every imaginable topic in record numbers during the 1920s, including several still in existence today.

One that went a long way in standardizing the culture was *Reader's Digest*. Its format included a compilation of articles taken from other magazines and rewritten so that they could easily be read in a few minutes, one a day throughout the month. It specialized in cheerful social observations, upbeat patriotic messages, inspiring dramas of triumph over adversity, and practical advice about successful living, all from an ethical and politically conservative perspective. *Reader's Digest* also included numerous one-or two-line jokes, one-paragraph humorous stories, and self-improvement vocabulary exercises. Printed in a smaller format than most magazines, it was suited for the bathroom or the bedside. And while its readers may have thought they were getting a convenient version of a wide sweep of American journalism, they in fact were receiving a carefully selected and constricted view of the world around them.

Other magazines included the nation's first weekly newsmagazine, *Time*, which covered a broad range of general news, from international affairs and science to religion and business developments. *Time's* relatively short, easy-to-read articles enable busy readers to stay abreast of their fast-changing world. *The Saturday Evening Post* emerged as one of the more popular magazines in the 1920s. *The Post* published current event articles, editorials, human interest pieces, humor, illustrations, a letter column, poetry (with contributions submitted by readers), single-panel gag cartoons and stories by the leading writers of the decade.

A number of magazines such as *Good Housekeeping* and *McCall's* catered to middle-class women by featuring short stories and serialized novels, recipes, dress patterns, and household tips. (In 2001 *McCall's* was renamed *Rosie* after its new owner Rosie O'Donnell, but lasted only a short time.) Other magazines, such as *Harper's Bazaar* and *Vogue*, focused primarily on clothing and fashions.

CALVIN COOLIDGE: Promoting Peace

The first American magazine to reach a circulation of 1 million readers was the *Ladies' Home Journal*. *The Journal* targeted married, white, middle-class women who took their roles as wife, mother, and homemaker very seriously. Each issue contained short stories, household and decorating tips, recipes, and advertised cosmetic, clothing, food, appliances, and other items seen as part of the woman's domain.

MAHJONGG AND CROSSWORD PUZZLES

Mahjongg and crossword puzzles also occupied Americans' leisure hours during the 1920s. Mahjongg is a game of Chinese origin usually played by four persons with tiles resembling dominoes and bearing various designs. These tiles are drawn and discarded until one player wins with a hand of four combinations of three tiles each and a pair of matching tiles. Mahjongg is thought to have been introduced to the western world via the English clubs of Shanghai, where it quickly gained popularity among the foreign residents. Joseph P. Babcock, the Soochow representative of the Standard Oil Company, was the first to import mahjongg tiles. To increase interest in the game, Babcock rewrote and published new and far more simplistic rules that became the American standard.

During this period, to meet the demand for production of new sets, cow bone was shipped from Kansas City and Chicago to Shanghai. In 1923, mahjongg sets numbered 6th in exports from Shanghai totaling in excess of $1.5 million. It would not take long for a number of American companies to also began producing mahjongg sets, Parker Brothers, United States Playing Card, and Milton Bradley to name a few. Before long, mahjongg was being played across the country with importers and retailers providing in-store demonstrations and lessons to help prospective players gain interest.

By 1925, the mahjongg craze was in full swing. The Jan. 25, 1924 issue of *The Saturday Evening Post* featured a cover illustration of a woman playing mahjongg, and the song, "Since Ma is Playing Mahjongg," became popular as sung by the noted Jewish singer and entertainer, Eddie Cantor. But, as is the case with many fads, interest in playing mahjongg died out by the 1930s, only to see a renewed interest in this century.

Although crossword puzzles date to 1913 in the United Sates, they did not gain widespread popularity until 1924. One day, two fledgling publishers, Richard Simon and M. Lincoln Schuster, visited Simon's aunt, who asked them if they knew of a book of crossword puzzles. They did not, but decided right then to publish one themselves. While single puzzles drew little attention, their Crossword Puzzle Book was an instant success. Each book came with a sharpened pencil—ready for action. Soon, enthusiasts competed in crossword puzzle tournaments across the nation, and the University of Kentucky offered a crossword puzzle class that was "educational, scientific, and instructive and mentally stimulating, as well as entertaining." By 1926, the craze had run its course, but crossword puzzles remain a daily feature of newspapers to this day.

OUTDOOR LEISURE ACTIVITIES

By the early 1920s, the automobile was so integrated into the American lifestyle, families turned to auto-camping as a popular pastime. Loaded down with collapsible baby cribs, tennis racquets, water coolers, picnic luncheon sets, thermos bottles, canvas tents, gasoline stoves, carbide lamps and telescoping camp cots, millions of Americans took to the road. In 1922, *The New York Times* estimated that of 10.8 million cars on the road, five million would be used for camping. At the peak of the touring craze in the late 1920s, before auto-camping was sidelined by the Depression, the American Automobile Association estimated that 10 million to 12 million motorists were taking an active part in the new pastime.

The first campers saw themselves as the daring elite. They experienced firsthand the trials and errors of the camping excursions on unpaved, and even non-existent, roads. And all too often, when the weather turned bad, drivers confronted notorious mud known as "gumbo," and rickety bridges.

Campers found out about parks and campgrounds by word of mouth from other campers. Through journals and articles, such as those published in *Motor Camper*, and hearing firsthand experiences from fellow campers, they were able to avoid disappointing vacations. Still, campers needed more information. Not only were the new camping journals inadequate sources of information, but maps were also lacking, if they were even available. As noted by Professor Warren Belasco, "road talk supplemented the incomplete information of Blue Books and maps."

During the mid-1920s, specialized camping trailers appeared on the market which folded out into a bed, kitchen, and shower. Other motorists pulled trailers, or "trailer couches," which served as both sleeping and cooking quarters. Vacationers of these trailers often referred to themselves as "tin can tourists," a nickname that had originally been applied to all campers due to the food they ate and the Ford "Tin Lizzies" they drove.

Originally, auto-campers simply pitched their tents and set up campsites along the roadside—often without obtaining an owner's permission. But as the number of campers grew, cities and towns along well-traveled routes began establishing municipal camping grounds to capture tourists' dollars and to prevent campers from damaging property. However, as the number of campers grew, it became too costly, even with fees, for towns to provide toilets, showers, electric lights, firewood, and drinkable water, thus many campgrounds were forced to close. In their place grew large campgrounds built specifically to accommodate both auto-campers, trailer coaches and emerging RV camping trailers.

COLLEGE FOOTBALL

Watching and following college and professional spots became, for the first time, the pervasive, consuming pastime that we know today. Prior to the First World War, college football was an exciting but minor sport, but as enrollments nearly doubled during the decade, the popularity of college football rose dramatically. As college football quickly became a large and powerful economic force, many universities and colleges constructed stadiums that held between 60,00 and 80,000 fans in hope of keeping up with the ever-increasing demand for tickets. Receipts for college football actually exceeded those for Major League Baseball and were used, in part, to pay coaches exorbitant salaries.

There are several reasons for the sudden attraction to the game besides enrollment. The sport had recently evolved from a strictly running game to a faster, more electrifying passing game. The game expanded beyond the eastern schools of the Ivy League to include large Midwestern universities such as Notre Dame, Michigan, Illinois, and many others bursting with talent. It was during this time famed coach Knute Rockne led his Notre Dame team to tremendous heights, including an undefeated 1924 season and Rose Bowl victory. Also, extensive radio broadcasting of games, and the showing of game highlights before a feature film, helped to contribute to the sports' growing fan base.

PROFESSIONAL BASEBALL

Professional baseball was dealt a punishing blow by the scandal that swirled around the 1919 World Series. In September 1920, eight members of the Chicago White Sox were indicted for conspiring to throw the 1919 Series against the Cincinnati Reds in exchange for a sizable payoff. Despite all players being acquitted, the newly installed first commissioner of baseball, Judge Kennesaw Mountain Landis, believing he had to do something to repair the damaged credibility of professional baseball, banned all eight White Sox players from the game for life.

While the Commissioner's edict aided in dissipating the mistrust felt by most spectators about professional baseball, Major League Baseball itself contributed significantly in drawing fans back. Until 1920, pitchers were permitted to scuff or alter balls with tobacco juice, saliva, mud, grease, and other foreign substances to make the pitched ball move erratically in the air and more difficult to hit. Then the League passed new rules forbidding pitchers from "doctoring" the ball. And when Cleveland Indians Shortstop, Roy Chapman, was struck in the head and killed, the League instructed umpires to replace dirty balls with clean ones throughout the game.

Another introduction made at this time was a tighter, harder, livelier ball that would not soften up as the game progressed. In earlier decades, so called the "Dead Ball Era," pitching dominated the game. Few extra base hits, and even fewer home runs, kept scores low, with the game confined to single hits, bunts, hit-and-run plays, and base stealing. But with a harder, more visible ball, which batters could now see better, baseball quickly became a high scoring game dominated by power hitters. And the player who would take the greatest advantage of these changes was a graduate of a Baltimore reform school named George Herman Ruth, Jr., or simply, "Babe" Ruth.

"In 1914, Babe appeared in five games for the Red Sox, pitching in four of them. He won his major league debut on July 11, 1914. However, due to a loaded roster, Babe was optioned to the Red Sox minor league team, the Providence Grays, where he helped lead them to the International League pennant. Babe became a permanent fixture in the Red Sox rotation in 1915, accumulating an 18-8 record with an ERA of 2.44. He followed up his successful first season with a 23-12 campaign in 1916, leading the league with a 1.75 ERA. In 1917, he went 24-13 with a 2.01 ERA and a staggering 35 complete games in 38 starts. However, by that time, Babe had displayed enormous power in his limited plate appearances, so it was decided his bat was too good to be left out of the lineup on a daily basis. As a result, in 1918, the transition began to turn

Babe into an everyday player. That year, he tied for the major-league lead in home runs with 11, and followed that up by setting a single season home run record of 29 in 1919.

"Babe dominated the game, amassing numbers that had never been seen before. He changed baseball from a grind-it-out style to one of power and high scoring games. He re-wrote the record books from a hitting standpoint, combining a high batting average with unbelievable power. The result was an assault on baseball's most hallowed records. In 1920, he bested the home run record he set in 1919 by belting a staggering 54 home runs, a season in which no other player hit more than 19 and only one team hit more than Babe did individually. But Babe wasn't done, as his 1921 season may have been the greatest in MLB history. That season, he blasted a new record of 59 home runs, drove in 171 RBI, scored 177 runs, batted .376 and had an unheard of .846 slugging percentage. Babe's mythical stature grew even more in 1927 when, as a member of "Murderer's Row," he set a new home run record of 60, a record that would stand for 34 years.

"The Babe helped save baseball from the ugly Black Sox scandal, and gave hope to millions during The Great Depression. He impacted the game in a way never seen before, or since. He continues to be the benchmark by which all other players are measured. Despite last playing nearly 75 years ago, Babe is still widely considered the greatest player in Major League Baseball history." (The biography of Babe Ruth is used with permission from the Family of Babe Ruth and Babe Ruth League c/o Luminary Group LLC., © 2011.)

* * *

The rapid expansion of commercialized leisure activities made ordinary people more sedentary. Instead of playing baseball or football, many people attended games to watch professional or college teams. Despite the increased opportunities to pursue a wider variety of recreational activities such as golf, tennis, or miniature golf, most people chose to entertain themselves primarily through activities that could usually be done sitting down. This new behavior also included sitting through movies or spending an evening around a radio. The decade of the 1920s introduced a lifestyle of passive recreation and leisure that continues to this day.

JAZZ

Much of the first section below comes from the public domain article A New Orleans Jazz History, 1895-1927. New Orleans Jazz web site. National Park Service; U.S. Department of the Interior.

It is not by coincidence that the decade of the 1920s has come to be known as "The Jazz Age." This was the time when jazz became fashionable, as part of the youthful revolution in morals and manners. Americans were now more urbanized, affluent, and entertainment-oriented than ever before. The music industry was quick to take advantage of the situation. In 1921, 100 million phonograph records were produced in the United States. Two years later production remained high at 92 million, setting a trend which continued until the radio became a common household item.

During the better part of the recording boom of the 1920s, Chicago was the place to be. The years 1922-1923 yielded a number of important recordings by two bands of New Orleans musicians who had come together in Chicago: the New Orleans Rhythm Kings and King Oliver's Creole Jazz Band. (It was the King Oliver's Creole Jazz Band which brought a young Louis Armstrong to wide public attention.) These two groups continued to use many of the elements associated with early jazz, such as stop-time, breaks, and ensemble riffing. However, they did much more with them, thus taking the concept of collective- improvised jazz to a higher artistic level.

Shifts in popular tastes began to undermine the influences of New Orleans style bands in a number of ways. Orchestras became larger, following trends set by Fletcher Henderson, Duke Ellington, Jean Goldkette, and Paul Whiteman. Star soloists took the spotlight, abandoning the collective approach to improvisation. Composers and arrangers controlled the balance between soloists and sections of instruments that supported them in the big band format.

The goal of every jazz musician is to find his or her own "voice," a sound that is at once unique and identifiable. One of the best examples is Louis Armstrong whose distinctive tone on cornet and personal singing style changed the course of American music. Armstrong's Hot Five was the vehicle for his growth as a jazz musician. In this group, he raised the New Orleans collective concept to unparalleled heights of creativity and then set a new direction with the sheer brilliance of his solo performances. Beginning in November 1925, the Hot Five produced almost three dozen records and revolutionized the jazz world in the process. Armstrong soon emerged as a star attraction, achieving popular success on the New York stage. Although his fan base was well established by the end of the decade, Armstrong's record company suggested he change suggestive (music and vocal) lyrics to avoid offending his white audiences.

Armstrong (left) and his Hot Five band

*   *   *

Paul Whiteman's Orchestra was the most popular band of the 1920s. The Paul Whiteman Orchestra rarely played what is considered real jazz today. While jazz purists accused him of diluting the character of jazz for commercial purposes, his superior dance band used some of the most technically skilled musicians of the era in a versatile show that included everything from pop tunes and waltzes to semi-classical works and jazz. And while his press agents dubbed him "The King of Jazz" in the 1920s, perhaps "King of the Jazz Age" would have been a better title.

Paul Whiteman began his musical career as a viola player for the San Francisco Symphony. He enlisted in the Navy during World War I, and his musical abilities resulted in the Navy putting him in charge of his own 40-piece band, playing march tunes by day and show music by night. Sensing new dimensions for popular music in the transition from ragtime to jazz, he organized a dance band and moved to New York in

1920. His initial recordings *Japanese Sandman* and *Whispering* were such big hits, selling more than two million copies, Whiteman became a household name. In 1924 he secured his place in history when he commissioned and introduced George Gershwin's *Rhapsody In Blue*. The song became the band's signature tune.

Whiteman's band continued its run into the 1930s, but toward the end of the decade their popularity began to wane. During the 1930s Whiteman hosted several radio shows, including Kraft Music Hall and Paul Whiteman's Musical Varieties, which featured the talents of Bing Crosby, Mildred Bailey, Jack Teagarden, Johnny Mercer, Ramona, Durelle Alexander and others. In the 1940s and 1950s, after he had disbanded his orchestra, Whiteman worked as a music director for the ABC Radio Network.

*   *   *

With the introduction of large-scale radio broadcasts in 1922, Americans were able to experience different styles of music without physically visiting a club or speakeasy. Through its broadcasts and concerts, the radio provided Americans with a trendy new avenue for exploring the world from the comfort of their living room. The most popular type of radio show was a "potter palm," an amateur concert and big-band jazz performance broadcast from cities like New York and Chicago. Due to the racial prejudice prevalent at most radio stations, white American jazz artists received much more air time than black jazz artists such as Louis Armstrong, Jelly Roll Morton, and Joe "King" Oliver.

In its early years, jazz faced resistance across America because it was considered a dangerous influence on young people and society. Jazz was different because it broke the rules—musical and social. It featured improvisation over traditional structure, performer over composer, and black American experience over conventional white sensibilities. Undercurrents of racism bore strongly upon the opposition to jazz, which was seen as barbaric and immoral. Yet, white youth from all social classes were drawn to jazz and the seductive new dances that went along with it. This newfound physical freedom, combined with the widespread belief that jazz stimulated sexual activity, caused critics of jazz to step up their efforts.

But the reformers couldn't fight progress. Jazz recordings and radio allowed the music to reach beyond the nightclubs and speakeasies, and with the sweet style of Paul Whiteman, gradually gained acceptance.

AVIATION

By 1917, the U.S. government felt it had seen enough progress in the development of planes to warrant something totally new, airmail. That year, Congress appropriated $100,000 for an experimental airmail service that was to be conducted jointly by the Army and the Post Office between Washington and New York, with an intermediate stop in Philadelphia.

With a large number of war-surplus aircraft in hand, the Post Office immediately set its sights on a far more ambitious goal, which was transcontinental air service. It opened the first segment, between Chicago and Cleveland, on May 15, 1919, and completed the service on Sept. 8, 1920, when the most difficult part of the route, the Rocky Mountains, was spanned. Airplanes still could not fly at night when the service first began, so the mail was handed off to trains at the end of each day. Nonetheless, by using airplanes the Post Office was able to shave 22 hours off coast-to-coast mail deliveries.

Three Martin MP Mailplanes await delivery at the Martin factory in Cleveland.

By the mid-1920s, the Post Office mail fleet was flying 2.5 million miles and delivering 14 million letters annually. However, the government had no intention of continuing airmail service on its own. Traditionally, the Post Office had used private companies for the transportation of mail. So once the feasibility of airmail was firmly established, and airline facilities were in place, the government moved to transfer airmail service to the private sector by way of competitive bids.

Congress's first step was to pass the Contract Mail Act, whereby President Calvin Coolidge appointed a board to recommend a national aviation policy. Dwight Morrow, later the father-in-law of Charles Lindbergh, was named chairman. The board heard testimony from 99 people and on Nov. 30, 1925 submitted its report. It was wide-ranging, but its key recommendation was that the government should set standards for civil aviation. This led to the passage of the Air Commerce Act of 1926 authorizing the Secretary of Commerce to designate air routes, to develop air navigation systems, to license pilots and aircraft, and to investigate accidents. In effect, the act brought the government back into commercial aviation, this time as regulator of the private airlines.

Henry Ford, the automobile manufacturer, was among the first successful bidders for airmail contracts. In 1925 he won the right to carry mail from Chicago to Detroit and Cleveland aboard planes his company already used to transport spare parts for his automobile assembly plants. It also would not take long for Ford to jump into aircraft manufacturing, producing the Ford Trimotor in 1927. Ford's *Tin Goose*, as it was called, was one of the first all-metal planes, made of a new material called duralumin that was almost as light as aluminum and twice as strong. It also was the first plane designed primarily to carry passengers rather than mail. The

Ford *Tin Goose* had 12 passenger seats, a cabin high enough for a passenger to walk down the aisle without stooping, and room for a flight attendant. Its three engines made it possible to fly higher and faster (up to 130 miles per hour), and its sturdy appearance, combined with the Ford name, had a reassuring effect on the public's perception of flying. However, it was another event in 1927 that brought unprecedented public attention to aviation and helped secure the industry's future as a major mode of transportation. Slightly before 8 a.m. on May 21, 1927, a young pilot named Charles Lindbergh set out on a historic flight across the Atlantic Ocean, from New York to Paris in his *Spirit of St. Louis*.

Charles A. Lindbergh was born on Feb. 4, 1902, in Detroit, but grew up on a farm near Little Falls, Minnesota. In childhood, Lindbergh showed exceptional mechanical ability. At the age of 18, he entered the University of Wisconsin to study engineering. However, after two years, he left school to become a barnstormer—a pilot who performed daredevil stunts at fairs. In 1924, Lindbergh entered a U.S. Army flying school at San Antonio, Texas. After Lindbergh completed his training in 1926 he became the first airmail pilot between Chicago, Illinois, and St. Louis, Missouri.

In 1919, a New York City hotel owner named Raymond Orteig had offered $25,000 to the first aviator to fly nonstop from New York to Paris. By 1927, four men had died, three others had been seriously injured, and two were still missing; still the prize had not been won. Lindbergh believed he could win if he had the right airplane. He persuaded nine St. Louis businessmen to help him finance the cost of a plane and chose Ryan Aeronautical Company of San Diego to manufacture a special plane, which he helped design.

Lindbergh's *Spirit of St. Louis* was slightly less than 28 feet in length, with a wingspan of 46 feet, and it carried 450 gallons of gasoline that comprised half its takeoff weight. There was too little room in the cramped cockpit for navigating by the stars, so Lindbergh flew by dead reckoning. The trip took an exhausting 33 1/2 hours, but he managed to keep awake by sticking his head out the window to inhale cold air, by holding his eyelids open, and by constantly reminding himself that if he fell asleep he would crash into the ocean and be lost forever. (Other pilots had crossed the Atlantic before him, but Lindbergh was the first person to do the nonstop solo.)

Lindbergh landed at Le Bourget outside of Paris at 10:24 p.m. Paris time on May 22. Word of his flight had preceded him and a large crowd of Parisians rushed out to the airfield to see him and his little plane. This was the first continent-to-continent non-stop flight in an airplane, and its effect on both Lindbergh and aviation was enormous. Lindbergh became an instant American hero. Aviation became a more established industry, attracting millions of private investment dollars almost overnight. The winner of the 1930 Best Woman Aviator of the

Year Award, Elinor Smith Sullivan, said that before Lindbergh's flight, "people seemed to think we [aviators] were from outer space or something. But after Charles Lindbergh's flight, we could do no wrong. It's hard to describe the impact Lindbergh had on people. Even the first walk on the moon doesn't come close. The twenties was such an innocent time, and people were still so religious—I think they felt like this man was sent by God to do this. And it changed aviation forever because all of a sudden the Wall Streeters were banging on doors looking for airplanes to invest in. We'd been standing on our heads trying to get them to notice us but after Lindbergh, suddenly everyone wanted to fly, and there weren't enough planes to carry them" (see Jennings and Brewster).

CONCLUSION

As the great Civil War historian, Bruce Catton, noted, the 1920s is the most misinterpreted era in modern American history. This is because so many of its popular interpreters became so fascinated by the things that floated about on the froth that they could not see anything else. "Most of the tag lines that have been attached to it are wrong."

In this short primer, it has been my attempt to delve beneath the froth and bring to light a more realistic view of the period. But even here I failed to some extent because there were many who did not benefit from the decade's prosperity or unparalleled consumerism. Much of the fanfare associated with the 1920s was enjoyed only by the rich and middle classes. In 1928, six out of ten American families made less than the $2000 a year, barely enough to buy the basic necessities of life.

Yet, much of what we take for granted today—forms of transportation, electricity, mass produced clothing, communication and entertainment, advertisements, leisure activities, male-female relationships, even how we find self-worth—arose during the 1920s. And even though no other decade was snuffed out so quickly, due to the stock market crash, the era of the 1920s saw the transformation of our nation from a rural to a modern urban nation.

SOURCES

Abels, Jules. *In the time of silent Cal.* Putnam, 1969. ASIN: B0006BYNKQ (Amazon).

Allen, Frederick Lewis. *Only Yesterday: An Informal History of the 1920s.* Harper Perennial Modern Classics, 2010. ISBN-10: 0060956658.

Baughman, Judith. *American Decades: 1920-1929.* Gale, 1995.ISBN-10: 0810357240.

Blanchard, Phyllis and Carlyn Manasses. *New girls for old.* New York, Macaulay, 1930.

Carter, Paul A. *The Twenties in America.* Harlan Davidson,1975.ISBN-10: 0882957171.

Davis, Ronald. *The Social and Cultural Life of the 1920s.* Harcourt College, 1972.ISBN-10: 0030841593.

Drowne, Kathleen and Patrick Huber. *The 1920s.* Greenwood, 2004.ISBN-10: 0313361630.

Dumenil, Lynn. *The Modern Temper: American Culture and Society in the 1920s.* AuthorHill and Wang, 1995.ISBN-10: 0809015668.

Goldberg, Ronald Allen. *American in the Twenties.* Syracuse University Press, 2003.ISBN-10: 0815630336.

Hanson, Erica. *A Cultural History of the United States Through the Decades - The 1920s.* Lucent Books, 1998.ISBN-10: 1560065524.

Hillstrom, Kevin and Laurie Collier Hillstrom, Editors. *The Industrial Revolution in America: Automobiles.* ABC-CLIO, 2006. ISBN-10: 185109749X

Jennings, Peter and Todd Brewster. *The Century.* Doubleday, 1998. ISBN-10: 0385483279.

Kallen, Stuart A. *History Firsthand - The Roaring Twenties*. Greenhaven Press, 2001.ISBN-10: 0737708859.

Kyvig, David E. *Daily Life in the United States, 1920-1940: How Americans Lived Through the Roaring Twenties and the Great Depression.* Ivan R. Dee, 2004.ISBN-10: 1566635845.

Lehman, LaLonnie. *Fashion in the time of The Great Gatsby*. Shire, 2013.ISBN-10: 0747812993.

Lynd, Robert S. and Helen Merrell Lynd. *Middletown: A Study in Modern American Culture*. Harcourt Brace Javanovich, 1959.ISBN-10: 0156595508.

McCoy, David B. *ENGLAND'S FIRST INDUSTRIAL REVOLUTION*. In Your Hand Digital Books. 2014.

Miller, Nathan. *New World Coming: The 1920s And The Making Of Modern America*. Da Capo Press, 2004. ISBN-10: 0306813793.

Moore, Lucy. *Anything Goes: A Biography of the Roaring Twenties*. Overlook, 2010.ISBN-10: 1590203135.

Mowry George E. *The Twenties: Fords, Flappers, and Fanatics*. Prentice-Hall, 1963.ASIN: B000OITP7C (Amazon).

Mokyr, Joel. "The Second Industrial Revolution, 1870-1914," *The Lever of Riches: Technological Creativity and Economic Progress.* Oxford University Press, USA , 1992. ISBN-10: 0195074777.

Nasaw, David. *Going Out: The Rise and Fall of Public Amusements*. Harvard University Press ,1999. ISBN-10: 0674356225

Pendergast, Sara. *U.X.L. American Decades (1920-1929).* UXL; 1920-29 edition, 2002.ISBN-10: 078766457X

Perret, Geoffre. *America in the Twenties: A History*. Simon & Schuster, 1983.ISBN-10: 0671251082.

Pietrusza, David. *The Roaring Twenties*. Lucent Books, 1998.ISBN-10: 1560063092.

Susman, Warren. *Culture as History*. Smithsonian Books,2003. ISBN-10: 1588340511.

Wukovits, John F. *The 1920s*. Greenhaven Press, 2000.ISBN-10: 0737702982

Zeitz, Joshua. *Flapper: A Madcap Story of Sex, Style, Celebrity, and the Women Who Made America Modern*. Autho Broadway Books, 2007.ISBN-10: 1400080541.

DVDs

Just the Facts: Emergence of Modern America - The Roaring Twenties. Cerebellum Corporation.

The 20th Century: The 1920s: A Decade of Contradictions [VHS] (2000)

On YouTube

The Century, America's Time: Boom To Bust (1 of 3)
http://www.youtube.com/watch?v=foooDFF9Dgs

The Century, America's Time: Boom To Bust (2 of 3)
http://www.youtube.com/watch?v=IJuEi-U6pmo

The Century, America's Time: Boom To Bust (3 of 3)
http://www.youtube.com/watch?v=sPP7FE8RIbY

WEB SITES

"Before electricity." The Institution of Engineering and Technology. 2013.
www.theiet.org/resources/library/archives/exhibition/domestic/before.cfm

"Listerine: past, present and future--a test of thyme." National Center for Biotechnology Information, U.S. National Library of Medicine
http://www.ncbi.nlm.nih.gov/pubmed/20621240

"Brief Costume History 1850-1919." Fashions of the Ages
http://www.fashionsoftheages.com/history1850_1919.html

"Radio". Encyclopædia Britannica. Encyclopædia Britannica Online. Encyclopædia Britannica Inc., 2013.
http://www.britannica.com/EBchecked/topic/488788/radio

A New Orleans Jazz History, 1895-1927. National Park Service; U.S. Department of the Interior.
www.nps.gov/jazz/historyculture/jazz_history.htm

Charles Lindbergh An American Aviator
http://www.charleslindbergh.com/

Aviation Resource Center
http://www.oocities.org/mkoop.geo/history/1920_1935.html

Commercial Aviation 1920 to 1930
http://www.century-of-flight.net/new%20site/commercial/Commercial%20Aviation.htm

SOME OTHER BOOKS BY DAVID MCCOY
- *The 1920s: Early Jazz and the Harlem Renaissance*
- *The 1920s: Margaret Sanger and the Birth Control Movement*
- *The 1920s: The Invisible Empire of the Ku Klux Klan*
- *The 1920s: The Scopes Monkey Trial*
- *The 1920s: Volumes 1 – 5*

- *Charlemagne: volume 1: Carolingian Dynasty Rise to Power and the Saxon war*
- *Charlemagne: volume 2: The Daily Lives of Peasants*
- *Charlemagne: volume 3: Becoming Holy Roman Emperor*
- *Charlemagne: volume 4: Carolingian Renaissance*
- *Charlemagne: Volumes 1-4*

- *100 Plus Ways to Protect Your Privacy*
- *The Average Family's Multi-Disaster Preparedness Manual*
- *A Short History of Hilton Head Island*
- *Gullah Culture: 1670—1950.*
- *Christopher Gist*
- *George Washington*
- *The Kent State Shootings and What Came Before*
- *An American's Guide to Understanding the Troubles of Northern Ireland*
- *England's First Industrial Revolution*
- *General John Burgoyne: general, statesman, playwright*
- *Moon Crater Shorty: A novella of Dada-like proportions*
- *The Military Career of General Lew Wallace: Mexico to Monocacy*
- *The 1898 Wilmington, North Carolina Coup D'état*
- *Andrew Jackson*
- *Francis Scott Key*
- *Oliver Hazard Perry: The Hero of Lake Erie*
- *Dolley Madison, Gilbert Stuart, and George Washington's Portrait*
- *The White Rose Student Resistance to Nazi Rule*

  - *The Discharge of Self: selected verse*
  - *The Sippo Lake Collection & Other Poems [nature poems]*
  - *Seeds of Change: three long poems.* "Seeds of Change" explores the changes that resulted when plants, animals, diseases, and people were exchanged between the Old and New Worlds as a result of Columbus's voyages of discovery.

Made in the USA
Las Vegas, NV
17 March 2022